Yesterday's Clearwater

VOLUMES IN THE HISTORIC CITIES SERIES:

Yesterday's CLEAR WATER

By Hampton Dunn

E. A. Seemann Publishing, Inc.
Miami, Florida

Abbreviations of photo credits used in the captions:

Anclote	Anclote Psychiatric Center
Burgert	Burgert Bros. collection, owned by Henry Cox of Tampa Photo Supply Company
C. C.	Clearwater Chamber of Commerce
Dunn	Hampton Dunn, Tampa
Mrs. Lamb	Mrs. J. C. Lamb, Tampa
P. C. H. C.	Pinellas County Historical Commission
Wyngarden	Lloyd Wyngarden, Dunedin

To
"COACH" J. A. THOMPSON
Vero Beach, Florida

my high school football mentor who taught his charges to play to win, and taught me a lot about how to tackle life itself.

Contents

Foreword

"Sparkling Clearwater" long has been known as Florida's "Springtime City" and is one of the state's most attractive communities. All through its infancy and formative years, Clearwater has appealed to young and old alike, to tourists and to natives. The beach is magnificent, the streets are clean, the climate is healthful, and homes and businesses are neat and modern.

It was a delight to dig up stories and photographs on Clearwater's past. When collected, organized, edited, and laid out, they add up to an impressive account of a Florida community which had its pioneer hardships, its halcyon days of the real estate boom, its sorrows of wartime, its sad depression years, its prosperous "population explosion," and its good times and bad. But people, nevertheless, found the town and later the city a beautiful place to live, to work, and to play.

Many people of the community assisted the writer in putting together this pictorial review of Clearwater, and to all of them I owe a debt of gratitude.

Here are a few: Henry Cox of Tampa Photo Supply Co., who made available to me the fabulous Burgert Bros. negatives covering much of the history of Clearwater; Ralph Reed, director of the Pinellas County Historical Commission; Al Hutchinson and the librarians at the *Clearwater Sun*; Mrs. Nancy Phelps at the St. Petersburg Historical Museum; the staff at the Clearwater Chamber of Commerce; Mrs. J. C. Lamb of Tampa; Lloyd Wyngarden of Dunedin; Dr. Samuel Hibbs of the Anclote Psychiatric Center; Judy Cowart of General Telephone Company, Tampa; William M. Acton of

[9]

Tampa, Clinton B. Conway of Clearwater, and the Jack Eckerd Corporation with headquarters in Clearwater. All of these people contributed invaluable photographs, post cards, snap shots, maps, memorabilia, and data.

Through such splendid cooperation developed *Yesterday's Clearwater*, a companion piece to the author's two other pictorial histories—*Yesterday's Tampa* and *Yesterday's St. Petersburg*.

HAMPTON DUNN

Clearwater, Florida
September, 1973

They Called it
Clear Water Harbor

During the time of the Indian wars in Florida, early settlers on the Pinellas peninsula found an attractive site for a community where a spring of sulphated water gurgled into the Gulf of Mexico, leaving its waters sparkling and crystal clear along the shore.

They called their new community Clear Water Harbor, a pretty name that was in use for many decades. It was Clear Water Harbor when the town was incorporated in 1891. According to the U. S. Postal Service, "Clear Water" became one word on January 19, 1895, and "Harbor" was dropped from the name on February 28, 1906.

But Clearwater's history goes back many centuries. What took the white man a long time to discover, the Indians had enjoyed since ancient times. There was an abundance of fish in the waters and game in the woods, the climate was pleasant and healthful, the scenery and surroundings were delightful.

Just who the earliest of inhabitants of this region were has never been pinpointed. It seems there were several strange races of men, some of them coming from the south from Mexico, some from the islands in the West Indies, or perhaps even from the far north by way of Alaska.

Because they left great mounds, the early people have become known as the Mound Builders. Many of the mounds were made entirely of shells, indicating they were refuse dumps of the shellfish-eating Indians. The white man, in modern times, put the contents of these mounds to use—to make shell roads.

SOME HISTORIANS SAY explorer Panfilo de Narvaez first set foot on Florida soil in Clearwater Harbor, others claim he landed around the Jungle Prado in St. Petersburg. In all probability, he did travel through the Clearwater area when he moved inland after anchoring on Good Friday, April 15, 1528. The author reads a handsome marker in Tampa's Plant Park. (Frank Hutchins)

The tranquil living pattern of the Indians was jolted on Good Friday of 1528 when a greedy, arrogant conquistador by the name of Panfilo de Narvaez set foot on the Point of Pinellas. Just where he stepped first is not really known and is widely disputed and debated by scholars.

Some historians, as St. Petersburg's Walter P. Fuller, vehemently claim that de Narvaez landed in the Jungle Prado area of St. Petersburg. But there are yet other scholars who firmly believe the explorer put in first at Clear Water Harbor. In any event, it is conceded that de Narvaez landed somewhere on the western shore of the peninsula and moved through the area that is now Clearwater.

The one-eyed, red-headed de Narvaez had lived an exciting life as an explorer and plunderer with Cortez in Mexico before coming to Florida. On his expedition here he brought five ships, 40 horses and 600 men. Also in the party were the first blacks to visit Florida. He antagonized the Indian natives immediately, and a natural enmity followed. De Narvaez and a party went inland by foot, sending their ships back to Cuba to be replenished with supplies. They were to meet their leader upstate at St. Marks. But they never reunited. De Narvaez and his few men built a crude ship and set out in the Gulf of Mexico where they perished in a hurricane.

[12]

Proud citizens of Pinellas very carefully explain that this area, then, was discovered ninety-two years before the Pilgrims landed at Plymouth Rock in 1620, seventy-nine years before the establishment of Jamestown, Va., in 1607, thirty-seven years before the founding of St. Augustine by Menendez in 1565, eleven years before Hernando de Soto discovered Tampa Bay in 1539, and just 36 years after Columbus discovered America in 1492.

Another famous Spanish explorer, Hernando de Soto, is also said to have landed in this area. A DeSoto Commission, appointed by Congress in 1935 to determine once and for all where DeSoto landed, came to the conclusion that he first stopped at Shaw's Point near Bradenton. A national memorial to commemorate the event stands on the south side of the Tampa Bay entrance. Other historians, though, have placed the DeSoto landing possibly at Pinellas Point, at Weeden's Island, or at Philippe Point.

A few years later, in March of 1567, another Spanish visitor came here, Captain Pedro Menendez, the discoverer and founder of St. Augustine. He came to the Gulf coast, searching for a water route across Florida to the Atlantic. The ferocious Timucuan Indians and their chief Tocobaga were getting a little annoyed by now with the invasion of the white man. Peace talks, however, brought on an uneasy quiet. Menendez left a few soldiers to establish a fort, but in a few months the soldiers were starving, and the Indians refused to give them food. In December 1567 Menendez sent a supply ship which found the fort burned and the soldiers massacred. The Spaniards, in retaliation, burned the Indian village and sailed away, leaving the Indians in sole possession of the Florida West Coast until the first half of the Nineteenth Century.

About that time, some fishermen ventured up this way from Key West and attempted to grow citrus trees here. But the Indians harrassed them so much that they gave up.

NAPOLEON BONAPARTE'S school mate, Odet Philippe, became head surgeon for the Emperor's armed forces, had a hectic career in the service, was taken P.O.W., and finally wound up in Florida. He heard glowing reports about the West coast of the state from a pirate he had treated. Thus he became the first white settler in the Pinellas peninsula, arriving about the mid-1830s. His grave is carefully preserved at the county's Philippe Park at Safety Harbor. (Dunn)

[13]

The Pinellas peninsula's first white settler was Dr. Odet Philippe, who had been tipped off to the wonders of this spot by a friendly pirate. In the mid-1830s, Philippe established his St. Helena plantation on the present site of Philippe Park. He supposedly introduced the first grapefruit in the United States, and is reported to have been the first grower to cultivate citrus trees in rows. Dr. Philippe had been a surgeon in the French Navy under Napoleon, a schoolmate of his. The site of today's Philippe Park, on the east side of the Pinellas peninsula, was at one time known as Philippeville.

Florida had become a territory of the United States in 1821, thus ending nearly three hundred years of Spanish rule (with the exception of the twenty years under the English from 1763 to 1783).

The confrontation between soldiers of the U. S. Army and Indian warriors resulted in a seven-year war that began in 1835. It was a costly, tedious conflict, and more than 1400 American soldiers gave their lives in battle. The Indians finally were driven into the Everglades, except for those who surrendered and were transported to reservations in the West.

The Army hastily built a network of defenses in many areas of the state. Fort Harrison was erected at Clear Water Harbor on April 2, 1841. This site was selected primarily for its healthfulness. Sick or wounded soldiers from other Florida forts were sent to Fort Harrison to recuperate. An average of 340 commissioned officers and enlisted men of the 6th United States Infantry were stationed at this fort during its occupancy. It was built on the

PINELLAS COUNTY PARK BOARD erected this historical marker at Philippe Park in 1945. It notes: "Here he (Dr. Philippe) raised a large family, many descendants of which now reside in Pinellas County. He pioneered in the development of this area and endowed this site with a history rich in colorful atmosphere." (Burgert)

DR. PHILIPPE'S GRANDSON, George Booth, is subject of this striking photograph. The surgeon's daughter, Melanie, married Richard J. Booth, a pioneer settler who had come over from England. The couple became the parents of the first white child born on Pinellas peninsula—Odet W. Booth, better known as "Keeter" Booth. (P.C.H.C.)

bluffs overlooking the beautiful harbor. A large log building housed the soldiers, and it was situated in the section now known as Harbor Oaks, at Druid Road and Orange Place.

Fort Harrison was named in honor of General William Henry Harrison, who later was to become President of the United States. The fort remained in existence only until November 1, 1841, when it was abandoned, since the Seminole war was about over and did end early the following year.

Even after the close of the war in 1842, some Indians still were on the warpath. Congress enacted the "Armed Occupation Act" which gave 160 acres of land to settlers who would come armed to live on the land for at least five years.

This act brought 24 claims from settlers in Pinellas County. One of these was James Stevens who was to become known as the "Father of Clearwater." Under his claim, he was awarded the lands and buildings of old Fort Harrison. In 1848 he received title to the land from the Government, covering all the territory west of Fort Harrison Avenue, from Drew Street south to Jeffords Street.

In the north end of Clearwater, a man by the name of Samuel Stevenson had settled in the early 1840s, and obtained his title from the Government in 1849. About 52 deeds were issued for lands on the Pinellas peninsula before the Civil War.

Pinellas historian Ralph Reed lists some other early settlers of Clearwater. The very first land claim on the Florida peninsula under the Armed Occupation Act was that of Elias J. Hart, in Hernando County. Hart moved to the Clearwater area with his wife, Margaret, in the late 1840s, where their son, William, was born in 1849. Hart's father, Isaiah Hart, was the founder of Jacksonville, and his brother, Ossian B. Hart, was Governor of Florida from 1872 to 1874, who died in office. Mrs. Margaret Hart, left a widow by the yellow fever epidemic, went through the Civil War with a large family of children to care for.

Richard J. Booth, a native of England, settled in Safety Harbor area after being discharged from Fort Brooks—now Tampa—in the late 1840s. He married Melanie Philippe, youngest daughter of Dr. Odet Philippe, and they became the ancestors of Pinellas County's large family of Booths.

Richard Garrison was one of the first settlers in the Dunedin area, around 1852. John S. Taylor Sr. came to Clearwater from Brooksville on a visit in the mid-1850s. He did not consider the land as valuable as that near Brooksville, and almost decided to return home without investing, when his friend, James Stevens persuaded him to buy his property in the south end of the city.

From a history prepared by the Clearwater Woman's Club in 1917 comes an interesting yarn on the price Taylor paid for his land. Just before he left his Brooksville home, his black cook (Taylor was a slave owner) had tried to poison his family by putting nux vomica in the coffee. Taylor, glad to get rid of the woman, gave her to Stevens in payment for the 160 acres of land west of Fort Harrison Avenue. Thus, the greater part of Clearwater once was sold for a black woman and, adds the Woman's Club publication, "a very unamiable one at that!"

The first free school on the peninsula was the old Taylor School on the Taylor homestead, built in 1855. Taylor later sold his property for $800 to David B. Turner and Robert J. Whitehurst, who divided it. The division line ran between the South Ward School house and the Methodist church. Some old orange trees on Whitehurst's piece apparently were planted by Stevens, but oranges were considered a worthless crop, since there was no market for them. Turner established the peninsula's first post office in August, 1859.

John C. White and family moved to the north end of Clearwater in the 1850s.

The first of the seven McMullen brothers, Capt. James Parramore McMullen, came here in 1842 for his health, and built a log cabin home in the early 1850s. He was followed by Daniel, Thomas Fain, William, John Fain, Malcolm Lawrence and David. McMullen is a name that is synonymous with pioneer, the good old days, and particularly, Pinellas County. At least one thousand descendants of the McMullan brothers now live in the county.

When these early settlers arrived, they found plenty of fish and game. It is said that during the Fall months, when the mullet were spawning, they often came to the Bay in such numbers that at low tide the men could walk out and kick them ashore, and the women scoooped up aprons full at a time. The roaring noise the fish made was often heard across the Bay.

But the pioneers had to work hard, and living in the area wasn't easy.

Natural disasters also marred the times. There was a vicious hurricane in 1846, and another in 1848, which was called "the gale of '48." The storm came with destructive force from the southwest and pushed the waters of the Gulf into Tampa Bay. All the islands and keys along the coast from Sanibel, at the mouth of the Caloosahatchee River, to Bayport, thirty miles north of Tarpon Springs, were inundated. Buildings were unroofed, and great damage was done in the Clearwater area.

Communications with the outside world was poor and slow. Some mail came by boat from Cedar Key. Most of it, however, was brought from Tampa by anyone who happened to go there. People usually walked, and often letters and papers lay for days in some households before reaching their destination.

The Civil War had much impact in Clearwater, and the young men responded to the call to duty. James P. McMullen organized a military company in 1861 and called it the Home Guards. Every man living in Clearwater became a member of the company, and many men from the surrounding countryside joined. Among those in the company were David B. Turner, A. C. Turner, J. D. Rogers, and William Campbell. After a few months, the company was disbanded and the men joined other Florida companies.

During the war, several gunboat raids occurred here with the invaders carrying away provisions and supplies of all kinds. The Woman's Club history notes that "many hardships were endured here, as in other Southern States. The women and children had, to a great extent, to provide for themselves. It was impossible to buy salt, and the half-grown girls had to procure it by boiling salt water. A large wash pot was taken to the beach and kept full of water, a brush fire built under it, and by night, two or three quarts of white salt rewarded them for their labors."

After the Civil War, local residents settled down to living in peace-time conditions, although the Reconstruction Era was as hectic here as elsewhere.

Clearwater got its first newspaper in the year 1873, the first in the Pinellas peninsula. The founding editor of the *Clear Water Times* was a minister, the Rev. C. S. Reynolds, who had emigrated from New York state and founded the *Tampa Herald* in 1854. He also was engaged in the newspaper business in Ocala, Palatka, and Key West—sort of a William Randolph Hearst of his day. He came to Florida for his health, with hope to live a few years longer. He made a remarkable recovery and did not die until 1904.

The Rev. Mr. Reynolds' newspaper gives us a good description of Clearwater in the 1870s. He wrote in the issue of August 23, 1873:

"Only a few settlers had established themselves on the peninsula found between Clear Water Harbor and the north arm of Tampa Bay, known as the Clearwater and Old Tampa settlements. These were engaged almost exclusively in raising and selling stock. The late disastrous war, which made such a total change in the structure of Southern society, caused a large number of persons to seek new homes and engage in new employments. The business of raising tropical fruits promised to remunerate those engaging in it, and those seeking proper location were pleased with the advantages which this peninsula offered. Surrounded on three sides by water, and with a large body of good rolling pine land with means of transportation by the waters of the Gulf, settlers were led to seek its promising offers and commenced to come in.

"The writer of this article, when on his way to his place, made a short stay at Cedar Keys, and inquired what was the prospect of business between Cedar Keys and this coast. The reply was that it would possibly reach two skiff loads a week. Now we have two schooners plying between these places, and several smaller boats regularly.

"We have good schools, churches well attended, and the most orderly population I have ever known. One fact speaks decidedly! Within the past five years there has been but one grand jury case in this western section of Hillsborough County.

"Within five years more the young orange groves which have been planted with other fruits that will be bearing, will make the residents of this section independently rich. Our lands are good and can be made rich. Our climate is almost unequalled. Our population is industrious and moral. These will insure prosperity. With the finest cotton, sugar cane, tropical fruits and rice, we have only to persevere for a few years and become independent."

The Rev. Mr. Reynolds also was a spiritual leader of the community in the early days who was the first pastor of the Midway Baptist Church that was organized on March 25, 1866. Later he supervised the construction of the log building to house the church.

The first organized school in Pinellas County was held in this log structure in 1874. The teacher was Jennie Reynolds Plumb, the younger sister of the pastor.

Midway Baptist was renamed Clearwater Baptist Church in September of 1878. In 1923, the name was changed once more to Calvary Baptist Church. Its sanctuary occupies today a prominent spot in downtown Clearwater, overlooking Clearwater Bay.

The decade of the 1880s was marked by many significant events and developments in the Clearwater area.

The period opened with a historic land sale in which the State of Florida sold four million acres at 25 cents an acre to Hamilton Disston and associates of Philadelphia. The land sold was supposedly "swamp and overflowed" acres, but there was some extremely fine high land included.

DOWNTOWN CLEARWATER featured this structure at the Northwest corner of North Fort Harrison Avenue and Cleveland Street in the decade between 1880 and 1890. The dressed-up gentlemen standing in front for the photograph undoubtedly were leading businessmen of the pioneer community. Old Dobbin, hitched to the wagon, was unimpressed with the picture-taking. (P.C.H.C.)

In 1881, former Governor Anson P. K. Safford of the Territory of Arizona, one of the associates in the Disston syndicate, came through this section, looking for a site for a large city. He could not find the land needed in the lower peninsula, nor was the required land available at Clear Water. He settled, therefore, on the high and rolling country along the Anclote River and Lake Butler and started what was to become Tarpon Springs, later the sponge fishing center of the Florida West Coast.

A lighthouse was built at Anclote Key in 1887. The structure was 105 feet high and the light was flashing instead of producing a steady beam as at Egmont Key.

As the decade of the 1880s began, Clearwater got its first hotel when M. C. Dwight arrived and bought some property to build the Orange Bluff Hotel near where the Presbyterian Church now stands. This hotel, along with several cottages built in connection with it, opened Clearwater as a resort of sorts, and a few tourists began to come. The Orange Bluff burned a few years later which was a serious blow to the town's tourist industry.

A little later a second hostelry, the Sea View Hotel, was built by Theodore Kamensky, a famous sculptor from Russia who fled when the Czar was displeased with a piece of statuary he called "The First Step" (toward liberty).

The most important development of the decade was the coming of the railroad to Clearwater and the Pinellas peninsula. It was the Orange Belt narrow gauge railroad which ran all the way from Sanford to St. Petersburg. It was promoted by a Russian immigrant named Peter A. Demens.

The promoters ran into serious financial difficulties, but Demens was persistent. "With chips and whetstone," he was said to have brought the railroad to Tarpon Springs where his money ran out.

W. L. Straub, former postmaster of St. Petersburg, a founder of the *St. Petersburg Times* and local historian, recounted an incident that happened during this crisis of Demens, in his *History of Pinellas County*, published in 1929.

Demens somehow had interested H. O. Armour of Chicago and A. J. Drexel of Philadelphia in his project, and the two financiers were expected on a trip to look over the railroad and the territory it was to serve.

L. B. Skinner, pioneer citizen of Dunedin, remembered being sent for by Demens and told his plan for imparting the right impression to the great capitalists.

"These are big fish," Demens told Skinner, "and we must catch them."

Skinner was to arrange for carriages to meet Armour and Drexel at Tarpon Springs and drive them through the fine lands to Dunedin, around that vicinity, and then to Clearwater—from whence they would be taken around to St. Petersburg by boat to avoid the flat-woods area north of that city. Straub wrote that the plan was carried out with success in all respects.

The indomitable Demens persevered, and finally on June 14, 1888, the first train of the Orange Belt Railroad came into St. Petersburg from the eastern end of the line on the St. Johns River. And Clearwater, St. Petersburg, and the Pinellas peninsula had a rail link to the outside world.

At the time of the coming of the railroad to Clearwater, only about eighteen families lived here. There were no paved streets and no improvements. A public dock had been built at the foot of Cleveland Street.

Meanwhile, other communities around Clearwater were springing up. Dunedin, which claims to be the oldest town on the West Coast of Florida south of Cedar Key, began in 1870 when a George L. Jones arrived at the small settlement and opened a general store. The town became known as Jonesboro. A few years later, two Scotchmen, J. O. Douglas and James Summerville, arrived and opened a general store in 1882. They petitioned the government for a Post Office and requested that it be called Dunedin, the Gaelic name for Edinburgh, which may be interpreted as "peaceful rest." Dunedin was incorporated as a town in 1889.

Although Largo had a few permanent settlers as early as 1853, it did not get a post office and railroad station until the coming of the Orange Belt Railroad in 1888. The name Largo was taken from a large lake, now drained, which was east of the present Pinellas County Fairgrounds. In 1905 the town

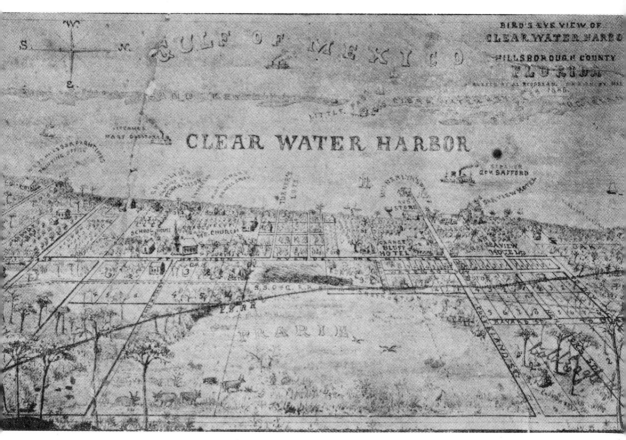

THIS BIRD'S EYE VIEW of Clear Water Harbor as it appeared in 1885 was published in a small history of Clearwater by the Woman's Club in 1917. It was prepared by Surveyor J. L. Rousseau and Cartographer B. W. Maddak. Along the waterfront, left to right, are: 1. Home of the *West Hillsborough Times*; 2. E. Purlin's orange grove and site of old Fort Harrison on the bluff at the former Brown estate; 3. Campbell grove; 4. Mary Turner's orange grove; 5. Turner's lots; 6. At foot of Cleveland Street, Munnerlyn's "Warf" and store with large building on end of dock; 7. Three-story Seaview Hotel, on bluff just north of Cleveland Street. In the bay are shown the side-wheeler steamer *Governor Safford*, just in from Cedar Keys, and the stern-wheeler steamer *Mary Disston* off the *West Hillsborough Times* dock. The small thin line at top is Clearwater Beach. (P.C.H.C.)

was incorporated and in 1913 it was either the second or third municipality in the country to establish a city-manager form of government.

The community now known as Palm Harbor was platted in 1888 with the name of Sutherland. In 1901, the town became the home of Florida Southern College which moved there from Leesburg and built a handsome complex of buildings. For twenty years, until the college burned in 1921, the town was alive with college students and their activities.

In the 1880s and 1890s, the little community now known as Ozona was an attraction for tourists. It originally was called Yellow Bluff but one of the visitors suggested that it be rechristened Ozona because he claimed the pure air restored his health. A popular resort in the town was the Magnolia Inn.

Historian Ralph Reed passed along some interesting observations of the growth of Pinellas County during the formative years by citing census figures from 1840 to 1880:

1840—All Hillsborough County, of which Pinellas Peninsula was a part, had only 452 residents, including 287 soldiers at Fort Brooke. On Pinellas, only Dr. Philippe and his family had settled although Captain William Bunche had a "fish ranch" at Mullet Key.

1850—Florida had become a state only five years before, in 1845. Pinellas Peninsula now had 35 families and a total population of 178.

1860—Pinellas had 82 families with 381 individuals. It had 22 vacant houses. There were 36 Whitehursts, only eight McMullens.

1870—The census showed 164 families; population 781. There were 42 Whitehursts, 37 McMullens, 25 Campbells, 16 Taylors, 14 Meares, and 13 Youngbloods.

1880—The Pinellas Peninsula was growing. The peninsula now could boast of 240 houses, and 1,111 persons. The McMullens had increased to 60, in 11 families. There were 45 of the Whitehursts, 15 Taylors, 10 Turners, 31 Meares, and 11 Archers. There were eight Booths listed.

With the coming of the Gay Nineties, the people in Clear Water Harbor were ready to organize. The town was incorporated in and received a special charter in 1897. The first Mayor was James E. Crane, a school teacher who served for four years. The first City Clerk was T. J. Sheridan.

In the first 81 years of existence, Clearwater has had only 31 different Mayors. The one who served longest was H. H. Baskin, with eight years, Frank J. Booth, George R. Seavy, and Herbert D. Brown each served six years. One Mayor was Ray E. Green, who moved up to high State office as State Comptroller

In 1895, the only paved streets were Cleveland Street from the harbor to

ORANGE BELT RAILROAD, which reached its destination at St. Petersburg in 1888, built this novel passenger station at Clearwater. Peter Demens, who built the railroad, used Russian architecture on all depots. If you look closely, you'll see an early train puffing away from the station while townspeople and new arrivals enjoy the excitement. (Clearwater Sun)

the small Orange Belt Railroad station, and Fort Harrison Avenue from Cleveland to a point south of the Methodist church. These streets were paved with shell removed from an old Indian mound near the harbor. In 1896, Cleveland Street was widened from 40 to 80 feet, and a clay road was built that year from the end of the shell paving on South Fort Harrison Avenue to the entrance of the Belleview Biltmore Hotel grounds at Belleair.

It was in 1895 that the comic strip railroad, the Orange Belt, became part of the Plant System. This was the operation of the fabulous Henry B. Plant who had brought his railroad over to Tampa and built the elegant Tampa Bay Hotel, which opened in 1891. Plant, a good operator, changed the name of the Orange Belt to the Stanford & St. Petersburg Railroad and, in 1897, installed standard gauge track. Finally, in 1902, the old Orange Belt became part of the Atlantic Coast Line Railway system which in recent years merged with the Seaboard Air Line Railway into the present Seaboard Coast line.

Plant was recognized as one of Florida's greatest nineteenth-century railroad developers and, more than any other person, was responsible for the growth of central and western Florida. During the 1880s and early 1890s, Plant had acquired a group of short-line railroads in South Carolina, Georgia, Alabama, and Florida, which he hooked up into a far-flung system.

Plant was also responsible for one of the most attractive landmarks in the Clearwater area, the fantastic Belleview Biltmore Hotel.

A historical sketch of the old hotel notes that "in those days it was fashionable for railroads to own hotels where important shippers and celebrities could be lavishly entertained, and whose patrons would help to create passenger traffic for the railroad. Mr. Plant's agents explored the entire West Coast in search of the ideal location for such a luxury resort. Seven years of research established that Upper Pinellas County enjoyed more days of sunshine per year than any other area."

The site of the hotel, on a bluff overlooking the bay, was first "discovered" by a sailing vessel captain, Charles Wharton Johnson, in 1870. He found it quite by accident; indeed, he was shipwrecked at the spot, liked what he saw, and moved his family there. The resort hotel was started in 1895, and construction continued through the following year. The Belleview opened its doors on January 15, 1897 to the wealthy vacationers who came from all parts of the world. It became popular overnight, a mecca of the railroad giants, steel magnates, utility kings, industrial barons, and socialites. It is the world's largest wooden structure that is still occupied.

When the Belleview opened, it had a small golf course, with six holes, with shell putting "greens." Henry Plant died in 1899 and his son, Morton F. Plant, actively guided the destiny of the hostelry.

Morton Plant was a golfing enthusiast who felt that this sport would play a big role in the future of the area. It had been universally believed that grasses suitable for golf greens would not grow in Florida and that sand greens were the only answer. But Plant did not accept that, and experimented extensively with grasses, soils, and fertilizers. Finally, he ordered entire trainloads filled with rich topsoil from Indiana and constructed a lush, green course. By 1915 the golf plant at the Belleview had been expanded to two 18-hole courses, designed by Donald J. Ross, dean of American golf architects. The Belleview attracted all the big names in golf—Bobby Jones, Henry J. Topping, Grantland Rice, Rex Beach, Irvin S. Cobb, George Ade, and Judge Kennesaw Mountain Landis, among the amateurs, and Walter Hagen, Gene Sarazen, George Low, and Tommy Harmon, among the pros. The women also came, including the incomparable Babe Didrickson.

Another sport at the turn of the century was bicycling, and many bicycle paths were constructed around Clearwater. At Belleair an asphalt bicycle race track was built where races were held each November, attracting some of the world's most noted riders.

Citrus-producing Pinellas Peninsula was badly hurt by the "Big Freeze" of

MORTON F. PLANT, a civic leader in his own right, was the son of railroad tycoon and developer Henry B. Plant. (P.C.H.C.)

1894-95. Some orange trees did survive, but some orange growers were discouraged and turned to other agricultural products, including strawberries.

At the turn of the century, several things happened around Clearwater besides its incorporation. J. N. McClung built the first ice factory here, in 1900, and this was to be the beginning of a water system for the community. He installed a water main from the ice factory to the corner of Cleveland Street and Fort Harrison Avenue. He further developed his system, and in 1910 the City purchased the plant from him. A year later the voters approved $40,000 in bonds for waterworks and sewerage.

The Clearwater Pier Company built a public dock and pavilion at the foot of Cleveland Street in 1902. A couple of years later, these facilities were donated to the City.

Telephone communications began in Clearwater in 1900, according to Dennis Cooper's history of General Telephone Company, *The People Machine*. John R. Davy, Sr., that year built a one-wire line connecting his orange groves near Safety Harbor with Coachman's Store in downtown Clearwater. The line came in by way of the D. C. McMillen homestead on the east side of town. Three years later, Davy built a telephone exchange to serve other residents of the area. A switchboard was set up in the home of L. N. Fowler on Haven Street with Mrs. Fowler as the first operator.

In 1905, Clearwater was illuminated when an electric light franchise was granted to J. N. McClung.

Business leaders formed a Board of Trade in 1905, a predecessor to the

Chamber of Commerce that came along years later. J. W. Williamson took the leading role in forming the Board of Trade. It was organized primarily to agitate for improvements in waterworks and sewers. An election followed and the necessary bonds were voted with 90 per cent of the electors favoring the proposition.

A spectacular fire broke out at 4 o'clock in the morning of June 24, 1910, that wiped out the entire business block on the north side of Cleveland Street, between Fort Harrison Avenue and Osceola Street. It's an ill wind that blows no good, however, and soon after the big conflagration, the Clearwater Fire Department was ready for occupancy. In the years immediately following, the City purchased up-to-date fire-fighting equipment at, according to the Woman's Club account, "large expense."

All these years, the Pinellas Peninsula had been part of Hillsborough County, widely separated from the county seat at Tampa and with poor transportation facilities. Way back in 1886, a pioneer citizen, W. A. Belcher, tried to get a county division act through the Legislature while he was a member, but failed.

Time went by, and in 1907, the gauntlet was laid down by W. L. Straub, editor of the *St. Petersburg Times*, who penned a fiery editorial which became a "Declaration of Independence" for Pinellas County. In it he forcefully pointed out why citizens of what was then known as "West Hillsborough" should have their own county. Copies of the editorial were put in the hands of every member of the Florida Legislature. Straub's main argument was taxation without benefits—Pinellas roads were badly neglected, for instance. The push was on, but steam did not build up sufficiently until the 1911 legislative session when John S. Taylor Sr., who was to become State Senator, and S. D. Harris lobbied for the division act in Tallahassee. The Legislature passed the bill on May 23, 1911, and it was signed into law by Governor A. W. Gilchrist.

The measure was, however, subject to a referendum which was held on November 14, the proposal carrying by a vote of 1,306 to 505. Governor Gilchrist appointed the first officials, and Pinellas County started operations in rented offices in downtown Clearwater on January 1, 1912.

Pinellas County's first officials were County Commissioners F. A. Wood and O. T. Railsback, St. Petersburg; S. S. Coachman, Clearwater; L. D. Vinson, Tarpon Springs; Jefferson Whitehurst, Anona; County Clerk of Court C. W. Weickling, St. Petersburg; Sheriff Marvel Whitehurst, Ozona; Tax Collector E. B. McMullen, Largo; Tax Assessor T. J. Northrup, St. Petersburg; Treasurer A. C. Turner, Clearwater; County School Superin-

MEET HIS HONOR, the first Mayor of Clearwater, James E. Crane, and his lovely First Lady, Mary Elizabeth Turner Crane, daughter of Clearwater pioneer Arthur C. Turner. Crane was elected when the town was incorporated in 1891. (C.C.)

tendent Dixie M. Hollins, St. Petersburg; County Judge LeRoy Brandon; Surveyor, W. A. Rousseau, Dunedin; Registration Supervisor Albert S. Meares, Anona; School Board Members A. F. Bartlett, St. Petersburg; A. P. Beckett, Tarpon Springs; and W. A. Allen, Largo; Justices of Peace William A. Hart, Clearwater; and J. J. Sullivan, St. Petersburg.

Then a big fight broke out over which city would be the county seat: St. Petersburg or Clearwater. The County Commission was controlled by residents of Upper Pinellas, who turned deaf ears to pleas from the citizens of St. Petersburg to change the site.

Historian Ralph Reed tells us: "Finally, the up-county Commissioners were served with an injunction, and, at a meeting on May 7, 1912, the Board, by a vote of three to two, awarded a contract to E. W. Parker, of Tampa, for a two-story frame courthouse, to cost $3,750. It was to be built within 30 days on lots given by the City of Clearwater on the present site of Peace Memorial Church. The building was guaranteed for two years.

"This first courthouse was built with volunteer labor, while the neighborhood women brought·food to the workers. Torches blazed around the rising structure as work went on through the night, and armed guards with shotguns patrolled it constantly, because rumors had been spread that St. Petersburg people planned to come to Clearwater and burn it down."

The first courthouse was used almost seven years. Its successor, scheduled for completion in 1917, was delayed when the original contractor went bankrupt because of World War I. The job was completed by others. It cost about $167,000 and in 1926 an addition was built on the northeast corner. Pinellas County outgrew its second courthouse by 1960, and a new building and jail were erected, adjoining the old one on the west.

Shortly after being formally organized, Pinellas County in 1912 voted a bond issue for $370,000 for hard-surfaced roads, and, four years later, $715,000 for brick roads.

The City of Clearwater continued to improve, voting in September, 1912, a bond issue of $40,000 for paving, pier construction, and Island Park upgrading. Two years later, another bond issue provided $75,000 for street paving and sanitary sewerage.

Congress allocated $29,000 to dredge Clearwater and Boca Ceiga Bays to Tampa Bay which was completed in 1915.

The city got a public library in 1916, under a grant from Andrew Carnegie.

Morton F. Plant was the benefactor who spurred the erection of a first-class hospital in Clearwater. In March, 1914, Plant put up a $100,000 endowment for such an institution, provided the community invested $20,000 more. The citizens raised their share, and the building was completed in 1915, named in honor of Morton Plant.

Civic pride shone through in this comment in the Woman's Club history recording the coming of the hospital: "It is one of the most beautiful and up-to-date hospitals in Florida. Situated in beautiful grounds, overlooking the Bay, it is an ideal place, the only drawback being that the people of Clearwater are so healthy that they seldom require the services of a hospital!"

In the year 1914, Clearwater received the services of a second railroad, with the coming of the Tampa & Gulf Coast Railroad.

Clearwater became one of the first communities in the country to extend women's suffrage. It came during a special election under a new City charter and was on the issuance of $10,000 in bonds to build a bridge across Clearwater Bay to the Island on the Gulf. A number of women voted on that election day, October 23, 1916, and the vote went 131 in favor to 9 against, on the bond issue. Miss Sue Barco was the first woman to cast her ballot.

[28]

THE GALLANT GUYS AND GALS who saved the town that night of October 30, 1891, when fire threatened to destroy the community. This was the dedicated "Bucket Brigade" who demonstrate here just how the system worked. (C.C.)

Pinellas County did its share toward winning World War I by giving men to the service, oversubscribing Liberty Loan and War Savings drives, generously responding to calls of the Red Cross, and making other necessary sacrifices. Clearwater had a company in the Pinellas County Guards which were organized in August, 1917. The unit, Company "D," was commanded by Taver Bayly.

The men had just returned from World War I and were beginning to settle down, when another calamity hit the area: The vicious hurricane of 1921. It has been described by some old-timers as "the worst hurricane I ever saw here."

The disaster struck on October 25. At 2 p.m. the barometer fell to 28.81, wind gusts reached 100 miles an hour and 6.48 inches of rain fell in a 24-hour period. The water rose to 10.5 feet above mean low tide, five feet higher than in any other hurricane since 1848. Ships were washed inland.

The storm roared in from the western Caribbean, swirled around Cuba, zoomed upward through the Gulf and made landfall about Tarpon Springs. This meant the Clearwater area got the worst lashes of the hurricane.

But happy days were here again as the zany Florida real estate boom became the next happening in these parts. Clearwater, like St. Petersburg and most other sections of Florida, was "active" as speculators began developing and selling property. Fortunes were made overnight. Streets, sidewalks, and other improvements were quickly installed. Tourism increased, as did the permanent population.

The beaches were popular. Clearwater replaced an old wooden bridge with the beautiful Memorial Gardens Causeway to connect the mainland with its superb Clearwater Beach.

But the big boom was short-lived. Its collapse was followed by the Wall Street crash, and then came a decade or more of hard times, an economic depression felt around the country as well as in Florida and in Clearwater. There were bank closings, and unemployment and soup lines and WPA and emergency relief projects of all sorts.

During the 1920s, the water-locked Pinellas peninsula did something about establishing links to the outside world. In St. Petersburg, a man with a dream, George S. (Dad) Gandy, went determinedly about building the long Gandy Bridge between that city and Tampa. It was opened in 1924 amid much fanfare and was an instant success, albeit a toll facility.

Meanwhile, Captain Ben T. Davis set about to building a nine-and-a-half-mile causeway from Clearwater to Tampa, the longest at the time built over water in the nation. Construction on the causeway began in 1927 and was completed in 1934, including a 3,510 foot bridge. It was opened to traffic on June 28, 1934. The roadway was 24 feet wide, smooth, straight, and well marked connecting Tampa and mainland with Clearwater, St. Petersburg, Indian Rocks, Pass-a-Grille, and other Gulf beaches. It was a toll facility that cost 50¢ for a round trip ticket, including passenger car and all passengers.

During World War II, in 1944, the Federal government forced both Gandy and Davis to sell their bridges, and then lifted the tolls. It came under the war powers act, since airmen from MacDill Air Force Base used the bridge and causeway to get back and forth to the base in Tampa, their temporary homes, and the recreational facilities along the Gulf beaches. Davis got $1,085,000 and Gandy, $2,382,642.

The Davis project was originally called Davis Causeway. But after World War II, the State Road Department widened and improved it and developed wayside parks along its approaches. The SRD then adopted the name "Courtney Campbell Parkway" to honor the local member of the Road Board, Courtney W. Campbell, who lived in Clearwater. The memory of Captain Davis is recognized in the name of "Ben T. Davis Beach" on the eastern end of the span, a municipal beach operated by Tampa.

World War II had its impact on Clearwater in other ways. The magnificent Belleview Biltmore Hotel was leased to the U. S. Air Force in 1942 for use as an auxiliary barracks for MacDill and Drew Fields in Tampa. As many as 3,000 Air Force personnel were housed at one time on the premises. The practice range and the first and 18th fairways of the West Golf Course were used as drill grounds. The hotel was returned to its owners in 1944.

A significant contribution to the war effort came from a prominent Clearwater resident, Donald Roebling, a multi-millionaire philanthropist and grandson of the builder of the Brooklyn Bridge. He was the inventor of the Alligator amphibian vehicle which was used extensively during WWII.

The big Roebling used to test his vehicle around the bay during the late 1930s and early 1940s. Historian Ralph Reed recalls the day he, Roebling, and the then-U. S. Senator (now Congressman) Claude Pepper were taking a spin in the tank. Roebling wheeled it up on land and the Senator took a spill.

President Harry S. Truman honored Roebling in 1948 by awarding him the Medal of Merit "for exceptionally meritorious conduct in the performance of outstanding service to the United States . . . conceived, developed, and perfected an amphibian vehicle capable of traversing both land and water, presented it to the government of the United States and released it for manufacture without compensation."

Almost as soon as the war ended, the West Coast, including Clearwater, began a fabulous growth and development that hasn't slowed down even into the 1970s.

Transportation and communications were improved. U. S. Highway 19 leading into Clearwater from the north was opened all the way, and most of it is now four-laned to the State line. And in 1954, another link to the outside world from the peninsula was created when the Sunshine Skyway, a modern engineering feat, was opened.

Pinellas County, which has been dubbed "Little Florida" because it is a sub-peninsula within a peninsula, in 1970 had more than a half million population, of which Clearwater had more than 52,000—and both are still growing!

A far cry, indeed, from the beginning days when this lovely spot on the West Coast of Florida was known as Clear Water Harbor.

Yesterday's Clearwater

Clearwater before 1900

IT WAS A BUSY CORNER in 1895, this spot on Cleveland Street, standing on Randolph's Corner. The left building is the new Bank of Clearwater. Third building on left is Rehbaum's Hardware. At right is the Coachman Building. (Clearwater Sun)

THE ORIGINAL PRESBYTERIAN CHURCH of Clearwater was on the site of the present day Peace Memorial Presbyterian Church. The church was organized in 1891 by the Rev. Luther H. Wilson. The lot for the church was donated by John R. Davey and his partners in business. The building was erected in 1895, and this photo was made in 1896. (C.C.)

PICNICKING WAS POPULAR in 1895, and it was inevitable that a group photograph would be made. This one was taken when the Ellis Musical Club got together on September 6, 1895. (P.C.H.C.)

Ellis Musical Club

THE OLD PUBLIC WHARF of Clearwater about 1895 at the foot of Cleveland Street before the dock house was built, and when the road was dirt and there were no sidewalks. In 1901, the Ladies Improvement Society was organized and among the enterprises for the public welfare in which this group was interested was the building of dressing rooms on the public dock, for the accommodation of bathers who did not have access to a private dock. (P.C.H.C.)

A TYPICAL HOME of 1890 in Clearwater was this dwelling on South Fort Harrison Avenue near the rail crossing. The frame structure featured fancy "gingerbread" carpentry. (P.C.H.C.)

RUSSIAN ARCHITECTURE brought to the area by Peter Demens, the railroad builder, may be reflected in this interesting structure on South Fort Harrison Avenue, north of Barry store. It was the home and studio of Photographer Louis Ducrois at Belleair in 1890. This picture was taken by Pinellas County historian Ralph Reed in the 1940s. (P.C.H.C.)

PROUD CITIZENS OF CLEARWATER pose in front of the first public pavilion and picnic shelter on the beach in the year 1898. They were heavily clothed to keep from burning in the brilliant sun. (C.C.)

AFTER HENRY B. PLANT acquired the Orange Belt Railroad and made it part of the Plant System, he built the gorgeous Belleview Hotel at Belleair. Here it is just after completion in 1896 (it opened on January 15, 1897) before the foliage and lawns had developed. The site high on a bluff overlooking the Gulf was discovered in 1870 by a sea captain, Charles Wharton Johnson. (C.C.)

THE BELLEVIEW HOTEL (later Belleview Biltmore) is the oldest operating golf hotel in the state. The multigabled hostelry (*above*) was a favorite of tycoons who flocked to Henry B. Plant's resort in their own private railroad cars, such as the two being drawn by this early locomotive in front of the hotel at the turn of the century. The rough golf tee (*right*) would invite moans and complaints today, but was quite an attraction when Plant himself played the hotel course, one of the oldest in the state. Donald J. Ross, dean of golf course architects, built two championship courses for the Belleview in the early days. (Dunn)

THE BELLEVIEW HOTEL TRACK was used both for bicycle and horse racing during the lively winter tourist season about 1898. The fabulous resort hotel has been in business continuously since its opening in 1897. (C.C.)

THEY WERE CHAMPIONS, this English bicycle racing team at the Belleview Hotel track about 1898. This was a popular sport of the day and attracted crowds from far and near. (C.C.)

UNIDENTIFIED EARLY SETTLERS of the Pinellas County peninsula. The two-wheeled cart is pulled by an ox, an early mode of transportation. The house is typical early Florida rural architecture. (P.C.H.C.)

ELEGANT FOR ITS DAY was the Phoenix Hotel (*above*) which housed transients during the early times of Clearwater. The neat picket fence added to its attractiveness. *Left*: Guests of the Hotel carefully posed for this photograph taken around 1900. (P.C.H.C.)

Clearwater from 1900 to 1919

CLEARWATER'S SECOND RAILROAD DEPOT in the early 1900s. The coming of the train always brought crowds to the station. On this occasion, the town's concert band is playing to welcome some dignitary. (P.C.H.C.)

TARPON SPRINGS in the early 1900s when living was easy in this lovely community to the north of Clearwater. (P.C.H.C.)

ONE OF THE FIRST MERCHANTS in Tarpon Springs was G. W. Fernald who built a store and dwelling on the north side of Tarpon Avenue sometime before the turn of the century. The store featured everything from shoes and clothing to hardware and groceries, as the sign indicates. (P.C.H.C.)

A HANDSOME RESIDENCE IN TARPON SPRINGS was this dwelling on Spring Boulevard. It has been identified as "Red Gables," the home of a Judge Rainstead. (P.C.H.C.)

LOOKING ACROSS SPRING BAYOU in Tarpon Springs to the beautiful Tarpon Springs Inn. The Inn burned in 1926. (P.C.H.C.)

SOUTH WARD SCHOOL (*below*) on South Fort Harrison Avenue (which later became the first home of Clearwater High School) was housed in this frame building in 1902 with an enrollment of 90 pupils. The group picture (*above*) came from Frank O'Berry of Lutz who was in the photo. The building was erected in 1883, enlarged in 1888, and again expanded in 1903 when it became a grade school. Its principal was Dixie M. Hollins who later became the first County School Superintendent when Pinellas County split from Hillsborough County in 1912. (P.C.H.C.)

A PIONEER MERCHANT was S. S. Coachman, a native of Georgia who settled in Clearwater in 1886 after stops in Lakeland and Webster. He had a sawmill on the site near where the Belleview Hotel stood. He built a general store, the largest in town, which he ran for 20 years. In 1894 he built one of the first brick buildings in the county. This is an interior view (*above*) of the S. S. Coachman & Sons

general store in 1902, at the present site of the Coachman Building at the southeast corner of Fort Harrison Avenue and Cleveland Street. Mr. Coachman later engaged in citrus growing. He was one of the leaders in the fight to separate Pinellas from Hillsborough County and became the chairman of the first Board of County Commissioners of the new county. He also served as a Clearwater city councilman. "Fancy Groceries" were delivered to the customer's doorstep by this wagon (*left*) in 1908. (C.C.)

[49]

THE CONCERT BAND performs on main street in the early 1900s. The wooden building is the old Coachman Store. (P.C.H.C.)

EARLY RECREATIONAL COMPLEX at the foot of Cleveland Street was a two-story dock house, pier, benches, and park. It was built in 1902 and quite popular. (P.C.H.C.)

THEY CALLED THIS THE CEDAR KEYS boat dock at Clearwater Pier because the vessels from Cedar Keys landed here and brought mail and provisions to the Pinellas peninsula in the early 1900s. The lower floor of the pavilion was used as a fish house, while the upper floor was reserved for dances every Saturday night. The boat in the picture is unidentified. (P.C.H.C.)

THE CENTER OF ACTIVITY in the early 1900s was the public dock and pavilion at the foot of the Cleveland Street hill. This was obviously a hot day, because all the nice ladies protected themselves with big, black umbrellas—suntans were quite unfashionable then. The street was still unpaved. (P.C.H.C.)

PRIVATE DOCKS in Clear Water Harbor in 1905. (C.C.)

DOWNTOWN WAS LIVELY in 1906—note the crowds on both sides of Cleveland Street, as seen here looking east from Osceola. (P.C.H.C.)

PLACID STREET SCENE in Clearwater about 1907: Fort Harrison Avenue with the old First Presbyterian Church on the left. No real traffic problems existed then! (Mrs. Lamb)

THE BANK OF CLEARWATER was brand new, it had just been organized in 1906, and Clearwater was on the move. (Dunn)

THE FIRST METHODIST CHURCH of Clearwater is one of the oldest churches on the Pinellas peninsula. It was organized about four miles out on the Tampa road as early as 1850, abandoned during the Civil War, reopened as part of the Brooksville Circuit and moved into town. In 1884 the Methodists erected a building of their own at Fort Harrison Avenue and Turner Street. This is the way it looked in 1908. This church building was in use until 1917, when a storm blew it down. (Mrs. Lamb)

PAVING FOR CLEARWATER STREETS! This crew's activity was good news for the town in 1910 when the paving of Osceola Avenue (*above*) and of the street by the railroad depot (*below*) began. The crews were deft at laying those brick, seen stacked alongside the station. (P.C.H.C.)

SOMETHING EXCITING WAS HAPPENING on Cleveland Street at Fort Harrison Avenue this day in 1910. It looks as if the kids were competing in some event. This was just before the big fire of June, 1910, which wiped out all the buildings in the upper left corner of this picture. (P.C.H.C.)

JUST BEFORE THE BIG FIRE in 1910: The North Side of Cleveland Street, west from Fort Harrison Avenue. Friend's Dry Goods Store on the corner later was replaced by the Peoples Bank. (C.C.)

THE BIG FIRE of June 24, 1910, razed all buildings on the North side of Cleveland Street from Fort Harrison Avenue to the house shown on Osceola Avenue. (P.C.H.C.)

THIS PATHETIC SCENE after the fire of June 24, 1910 shows smoke shrouding the area on the North side of Cleveland Street, from Osceola Avenue. Soon afterwards a volunteer fire department was formed. In 1914, the City purchased adequate fire equipment. (P.C.H.C.)

THE NEW DEPOT, Clearwater's second, was an exciting place to be back there in 1910. Automobiles were appearing on the scene about that time. (Clearwater Sun)

THE CITY REBUILT after the Big Fire of 1910. This is Fort Harrison Avenue looking north from Cleveland Street. The Peoples Bank, now the First National Bank, was built at the present site of Wolf Bros. store. The Jeffords-Smoyer Store stands on the northeast corner where the Bank of Clearwater was built later. (P.C.H.C.)

HOME OF the *Clearwater News* on Cleveland Street. The newspaper was founded in 1893 by the Rev. C. S. Reynolds, the same man who had published the *Clear Water Times* 20 years before. In 1913, a stock company was formed with C. H. Evans as editor. In 1921, it was turned into a morning daily. In 1925, it became the *Morning Herald* and continued as such until 1927, when the then-owner, Frank F. Pulver, of St. Petersburg, sold it to the *Sun* Company. (P.C.H.C.)

A "LAUNDERETTE" in the early days when local folk boiled their clothes in a wash pot to help get rid of the dirt. It was a hot and tiring job, doing the laundry by hand. (P.C.H.C.)

[58]

CANE-GRINDING TIME in Pinellas presented this scene. The boys were on hand, eager to drink the delicious cane juice that oozed from the stalks as they were crushed. (P.C.H.C.)

THE 1911 CLASS of the Ozona School near Clearwater. Ozona is one of the oldest communities in the county. "Uncle Walton" Whitehurst came here in 1868 and "took up" State land in what was known to the spongers, fishermen, and Cubans as "Yaller Bluff." When the tourists started coming here after the Orange Belt Railroad was built, townspeople changed the name to Ozona—anything "yellow" in those days suggested yellow fever and gave the place a bad image. (P.C.H.C.)

THE J. W. SUTTLE GROCERY at the corner of North Garden and Hendrix in the year 1912. Mr. Suttle is seen standing at the left of the photo. This was the typical way grocery stores displayed their wares in the early days, including produce in crates and baskets. (C.C.)

ERECTED ALMOST OVERNIGHT in 1912 to save the county seat for Clearwater, this small frame two-story structure (which site is now occupied by Peace Memorial Church) served as the first court house for Pinellas County when it split away from Hillsborough. Pictured in front of the building are most of the infant county's first officers. They are: School Board—W. A. Allen, Clearwater; A. F. Bartlett, St. Petersburg; A. P. Beckett, Tarpon Springs; and Dixie M. Hollins, County School Superintendent. C. W. Weickling, St. Petersburg, Clerk of Court. Marvel M. Whitehurst, Clearwater, Sheriff. LeRoy Brandon, County Judge. J. T. Northrup, Tax Assessor. E. B. (Uncle Eli) McMullen, Tax Collector. A. C. Turner, Treasurer. Albert S. Meares, Supervisor of Registration. W. R. Rousseau, Surveyor. (Clearwater Sun)

Facing page: EARLY DUNEDIN near Clearwater. Some of the people standing in front of the Douglas and Sommerville store have been identified as Charles H. Gilchrist (man in shirt sleeves), Mrs. J. R. Brumby (on his left), and Miss Fanny Patton (in door with white waist). John O. Douglas and James Sommerville came to Dunedin from Scotland in 1882 and established a store at the foot of Main Street in Edgewater Park. Gilchrist came to Dunedin in 1902 and opened a general store in 1903, in the building formerly operated by Douglas and Sommerville. (P.C.H.C.)

CLEARWATER'S CITY HALL and Fire Department in 1915. The new pumper is in front of the fire house. Fire Chief Ora Hart is the man in the white coat. Firemen include Bill McKillup, Walter Lovell, Shorty Mitchell, Joe Russell, Art Geiselman and George Bolton. (Clearwater Sun)

THE PINELLAS COUNTY HOME GUARDS were organized in August, 1917, following a call by President Wilson for such organizations to protect the states after the country entered World War I. Clearwater formed Company D with Taver Bayly as commander. The Guards were fully armed and equipped and drilled regularly. Besides affording protection to the county, the Pinellas County Guards were instrumental in the arrest of 22 spies during the war. (P.C.H.C.)

MORTON F. PLANT HOSPITAL was built in 1914 with a $100,000 endowment by Henry Plant's son and with $20,000 matching funds raised by the citizens. The original hospital contained two wards an; some private rooms with a total of 21 beds. (C.C.)

OLD WOODEN EPISCOPAL CHURCH on South Fort Harrison Avenue in 1915. The Rev. A. T. Cornwell was rector at the time. The Church of the Ascension was built about 1883 on the northwest corner of Fort Harrison and Haven Street where the County Court House was erected later. A small frame building at first, it was twice enlarged and once moved. The church property was sold in 1924, and a new building begun elsewhere. (C.C.)

THIS WAS THE MAIN HIGHWAY into Clearwater from the east, Coachman Station, in 1915. Citizens voted a $715,000 bond issue for 75 miles of a nine-foot wide brick road on sand. This modern road was completed in 1917. When two cars met, each would slow down and pull off the brick with two wheels to pass. (C.C.)

[64]

THE "BEST IN TOWN" was the Grey Moss Inn, the former Verona Inn. (P.C.H.C.)

IT WAS A RED LETTER DAY for Pinellas County in 1916 when the first train rumbled to Indian Rocks Beach. (P.C.H.C.)

DR. BETHEL McMULLEN (*at right*) of the Pinellas McMullens was a veteran of the Confederate Army. He is shown here talking to another veteran. He was a son of pioneer James McMullen. (P.C.H.C.)

TWO YOUNG SOCIALITES of Clearwater in 1917, Katharine Bird and Alice Dillard, are mounted for an afternoon of horseback riding. (P.C.H.C.)

MANDALAY ROAD on Clearwater Beach was still unpaved in 1920, and many vehicles got stuck here. (C.C.)

Facing page: AS THE ROARIN' TWENTIES began, Pinellas County began to get some paved highways. This road ran underneath spreading limbs of gigantic oaks near Safety Harbor. (Burgert)

Clearwater in the 1920s

BASEBALL WAS POPULAR in the Twenties—this is the waterfront baseball field in 1920. (P.C.H.C.)

AN EARLY JITNEY BUS, a 12-passenger Ford, ran between Clearwater, Largo, Dunedin, and St. Petersburg. This picture was taken at Largo in front of the New Pinellas Hotel. (P.C.H.C.)

HOMES NESTLE AMID GREENERY in this Clearwater panorama of June 1921, the beginning of the swinging days of the gala decade. (P.C.H.C.)

THE NEW PAVILION at Clearwater Beach attracted huge crowds in 1921. It was razed in the 1930s. (Burgert)

BUSY DOWNTOWN at Cleveland Street in 1921. Note the jitney bus, third from right, which commuted between Clearwater and Clearwater Beach. (Burgert)

THE DELIGHTFUL CLEARWATER BEACH HOTEL was packing 'em in in 1921. It is still standing and doing business in the 1970s. (Burgert)

CAPTIVATING ANCLOTE RIVER near Tarpon Springs typifies Florida's natural beauty at its best. (Burgert)

SOUTHERN COLLEGE OCCUPIED this handsome structure in 1920 at Sutherland (now Palm Harbor). A few months later, on January 29, 1921, fire destroyed the magnificent dormitory for women and the administration building of the Methodist-oriented institution. The College was established in 1883 in Orlando as "Wesleyan Institute" by the Florida Methodist Conference; was removed to Leesburg in 1886 as "The Florida Conference College" (with four teachers and 58 students); and to Sutherland in 1902, where it was renamed the Florida Seminary. In the crisis after the fire, E. T. Roux offered his splendid hotel at Clearwater Beach for exclusive use as temporary quarters for the college. The following year it was renamed Florida Southern College and moved to Lakeland where it continues to operate. (Burgert)

SOUTHERN COLLEGE AFTER THE BIG FIRE in 1922. What was left became the Clearwater Beach Hotel. (C.C.)

THE EPISCOPAL CHURCH OF THE ASCENSION in Clearwater in 1922 was located at the corner where the Court House now stands. It was built in 1883 and enlarged several times before the property was sold in 1924. (Burgert)

IT WAS SEABOARD AIR LINE RAILWAY when this picture of the Clearwater passenger station on Court Street was taken in 1922. Eventually, Seaboard was merged with the Atlantic Coast Line Railroad under the name Seaboard Coast Line. This station is still in use. (Burgert)

THE SPONGE INDUSTRY, which once flourished off Key West, moved to Tarpon Springs during the Spanish American War of 1898 because of the spongers' fear of Spanish warships. From this small beginning developed the Tarpon Springs Sponge Exchange (shown above on a busy day in 1921). At first, the boats came here from Key West, but in 1905 divers were brought to Tarpon Springs by John K. Cheney. John Corcoris, an employee of Cheney's and the first Greek to come to Tarpon Springs, convinced his employer to bring in Greek divers from the Mediterranean in order to expand the sponge industry. Here's another look inside the Sponge Exchange (*below*) when bidding was lively for the prized products. (Burgert)

GREEKS HAVE BEEN SPONGERS as far back as recorded history. The sponge, an article of commerce since long before the Christian era, is the skeleton of an animal that adheres to the bottom of the sea, a rock, or a coral reef. Sponges were first found in the Mediterranean Sea and are mentioned in the Bible as well as in the literature of Ancient Greece. This photograph is of a sponge boat captain in the early 1920s. (Burgert)

SUCH NAMES as *Socrates* decorate the sponge boat fleet in the 1920s. The industry flourished, and at one time there were as many as 1,200 spongers here. But about 1947 a blight, the red tide, brought sponging activity to a standstill. The steady decline of the sponge industry since has been accelerated by the introduction of synthetic sponges. But there is still a limited demand for natural sponges. (Burgert)

STILL NEAT AND ATTRACTIVE in 1922 was the old Phoenix Hotel at Cleveland Street and Garden Avenue. It was later demolished after catering to Clearwater visitors for many years. (Burgert)

THIS LOVELY HOME in Harbor Oaks typifies the architecture of the year 1922. It still stands and is presently occupied by Clearwater attorney Chester B. McMullen, Jr. (Burgert)

THEN, AS NOW, the Coachman Building in downtown Clearwater at Cleveland Street and Fort Harrison Avenue was the center of attraction in 1922. (Burgert)

[78]

THIS AERIAL VIEW of 1923 shows Clearwater's fine Junior High School (*in rear*) and Senior High School (*in front*) on North Greenwood Avenue, corner of Laura Street. (P.C.H.C.)

PINELLAS COUNTY COURT HOUSE in the 1920s. The fine facility was erected in 1918 and is still in public service for the county. There is now a modern annex that houses most county administrative offices, except for a few. The Pinellas County Historical Commission, headed by historian Ralph Reed, operates here an outstanding historical museum. (P.C.H.C.)

THE DUNEDIN FIRE DEPARTMENT sported this up-to-date equipment in 1923, the fire truck in front, with a Model T Ford truck in the rear. Dunedin dates back to 1868 when the Rev. Joseph Brown and family of Virginia pioneered here. A few years later, George L. Jones opened a general store, and the community became known as Jonesboro. But that name was short-lived, as some Scotsmen came over and began development here. They were natives of Dunedin, Scotland, and they transferred the name here. The Florida town claimed to be the "Eden on the Gulf." (P.C.H.C.)

GUARANTEE TITLE AND TRUST COMPANY occupied this building in 1924. It subsequently was acquired by the City of Clearwater and served as the home of the Chamber of Commerce from 1935 to 1964. (C.C.)

CALVARY BAPTIST CHURCH was under construction in 1924 (*above*). The church was organized as Midway Baptist Church on March 25, 1866, by the Rev. C. S. Reynolds and several followers, 35 years before the incorporation of Clearwater. Midway was renamed Clearwater Baptist in 1878, and Calvary Baptist in 1923. *Below*: Calvary Baptist upon completion at Cleveland and Osceola Streets in downtown Clearwater. Miss Elizabeth A. Whitmire, a winter resident from Greenville, South Carolina, with a dream of a church overlooking the water, purchased the present site of the church in 1920 for $15,000 in cash. She worked secretly with the then-pastor A. J. Kroelinger to build the church and pledged $117,500 for construction. No one except the pastor knew her identity until after her death in 1928. (Burgert)

THE ELEGANT GREY MOSS INN on South Fort Harrison Avenue in 1924. Fords were the popular vehicle in the Roarin' Twenties, as evidenced here. (Burgert)

CLEARWATER'S "HOME-LIKE HOTELS" was the description given such places as the Sea Ora Lodge on North Osceola Avenue. (P.C.H.C.)

INDIAN ROCKS BEACH at its finest—when it is filled with splashing, fun-seeking bathers. This photograph was made on July 21, 1925, in the heat of the summer season. (Burgert)

THE NEW PAVILION at Clearwater Beach was exceedingly busy on July 21, 1925, when the [83] photographer was making the rounds of Gulf beaches. Many of the gentlemen out on the pier were dolled up with coats, ties, and skimmer hats. (Burgert)

DOWNTOWN CLEARWATER at Cleveland Street and North Fort Harrison Avenue. (Clearwater Sun)

THE BANK OF CLEARWATER at Cleveland Street and Fort Harrison Avenue has long dominated the downtown scene. That's Woods Jewelry on the right and H. G. Smith Hardware in the background. The bank was the city's oldest and largest and was organized in 1906 with $18,000 capital stock. D. F. Conely served as the first president. (Burgert)

Facing page: PRETTY LITTLE GIRLS with bows in their hair stroll alongside a country road near Safety Harbor in the mid-1920s. The Ford chugs along over the nine-foot brick road, considered excellent in its day. (Burgert)

[84]

THE CLEARWATER BOWLING CLUB at the City Park in the mid-1920s. (P.C.H.C.)

[86] THE BEAUTIFUL SUNSET HILLS Country Club at Tarpon Springs was one of the finest golf layouts on the Florida West coast during the real estate boom of the 1920s. The club was built at the height of the real estate promotion and operated an 18-hole course on its 120 acre tract. (Anclote)

EXCLUSIVE HARBOR OAKS
SUBDIVISION of Clearwater featured
beautiful homes such as this. It is owned
now by former Assistant U.S. Attorney
Frank Muscarella. (Burgert)

LONG DRESSES WERE IN STYLE with these young
ladies who took advantage of scenic surroundings to
take pictures. This is South Druid Road at the south
entrance to Harbor Oaks in Clearwater. (Burgert)

A SAND ROAD snakes through the Crest Lake area of
Clearwater and offers a pretty setting to enjoy Florida
living. (Burgert)

AMERICA'S HEALTHIEST GIRL was the center of attraction at this gathering of beauty champions during the 1920s. She was Miss Florence Smock of Eustis, Fla. The "Miss America" was Miss Margaret Eckdahl of Tampa. Identity of the other beauties not available. At right are Mayor H. H. Baskin of Clearwater and R. B. Norton, president of the Clearwater Chamber of Commerce. (P.C.H.C.)

CHARTER MEETING of the Clearwater Pioneer Pelican Club on a boat south of the Seminole Street Bridge in 1925. The birds are familiar to residents and visitors in the Springtime City. (P.C.H.C.)

Preceding page: CLEARWATER FROM THE AIR in 1925. There was a lot of room for development yet! (P.C.H.C.)

along the State road east of Clearwater when this photo was made. Note the sharp curve that typified highways of the day. (P.C.H.C.)

SAFETY HARBOR (*above*) was once called Espiritu Santo, or Spring of the Holy Spirit. It's a pleasant community on a high bluff overlooking Old Tampa Bay, only seven miles away from Clearwater. At one time the town was also known as Green Springs on account of the remarkable recovery of a Dr. Green whose paralysis was supposedly cured by the spring water. *Below* is a view of Safety Harbor from the water. (Burgert)

DOWNTOWN SAFETY HARBOR during the Florida real estate boom in 1926. (Burgert)

GIRL WATCHERS and shapely bathers alike enjoy the pool at the old Safety Harbor Spa, even in winter, as this picture shows which was taken on December 6, 1925. The town is famed as "The Health-Giving City," a city "where the Healing Waters flow." (Burgert)

WELCOME TO OLDSMAR is the message of this large billboard on the narrow highway leading into the town. Oldsmar had its beginning in 1917, when Ransom E. Olds, pioneer automobile manufacturer of Lansing, Mich., came into possession of 37,500 acres of land situated on Old Tampa Bay, partly in Hillsborough and partly in Pinellas Counties. The inventor and manufacturer of one of America's first automobiles, the "Reo," from his initials, later named the "Oldsmobile," envisioned a city around his newly-founded tractor plant. More than 1,000 Lansing neighbors shared his vision and moved their homes and families to the infant "Oldsmar," planning to settle their land for generations. (Burgert)

[93]

BATHING BEAUTIES helped to publicize Oldsmar during the Florida boom and here was a trademark pointing up the town as the suburb to two cities—Tampa and St. Petersburg. No Clearwater? (Burgert)

THE OLDSMAR BANK in 1925 housed the Woman's Club, the Board of Trade, the Oldsmar Growers Association, the Public Library, the Boy Scouts, the Odd Fellows Lodge, and the Masonic Lodge. (Burgert)

THE OLDSMAR GARAGE in 1924 kept busy repairing automobiles of the day, including the recharging of Ford magnetos. Within a few short years, the depression squeezed out the Olds Farm Tractor Factory and left many homeless and unemployed. The town was deserted for awhile, then blossomed again during the real estate boom under the name Tampashores. (Burgert)

THE WAYSIDE INN, also known at times as the Olds Tavern, offered visitors room and board for $15-$20 a week and was a popular spot for dining, drawing crowds from Tampa and other area locales. Just across the street from the Wayside was a public park with orchestra concerts for the public every Sunday afternoon. A fleet of 42 buses ran daily from Oldsmar to attractions in the area, free of charge. Finally, the Wayside Inn burned down. (Burgert)

BOOM-TOWN OLDSMAR staged barbecues in mid-winter to attract large crowds interested in investing in the revived community. They wore their top coats and queued up for free chow. (Burgert)

GALS AND FLOWERS bedecked the good-looking float advertising Oldsmar in the Gasparilla Parade in Tampa in 1925. The Oldsmar development was being pushed by real estate man Harry E. Prettyman. (Burgert)

THERE WERE MID-WINTER GAMES to entertain the folks in Oldsmar during the boom. Here's some of the activity in front of the popular Wayside Inn. They called Oldsmar "The Wonder Town of Pinellas." (Burgert)

THEY DRILLED FOR OIL in Oldsmar which brought curiosity seekers to the community near Clearwater. (Burgert)

ANOTHER ATTENTION-GETTER in advertising Oldsmar was this prairie schooner which roamed around the country promoting R. E. Olds' boom town. (Burgert)

CARS WERE PARKED DIAGONALLY on both sides of the street in downtown Clearwater during the hectic days of the Florida real estate boom in 1926. (General Telephone Co.)

CHANGING THE SKYLINE OF CLEARWATER in 1926 was the skyscraper Fort Harrison Hotel which became and has remained ever since a popular hostelry. It's on Fort Harrison Avenue. (Burgert)

THE TASTEFULLY DECORATED
LOBBY of the Fort Harrison Hotel
(*above*) has been a favorite meeting place
for friends since the hotel opened in
1926. The nicely furnished card room
(*left*) and the Skyline Room (*bottom
left*) are good examples of the hospital-
ity and entertainment offered by the
hotel. (Burgert)

THIS WAS THE CLEARWATER YACHT CLUB on the mainland in 1928, on the present site of the band shell just west of Maas Bros. Store. (C.C.)

THE GREY GULL INN, owned by Carl Stig, as it appeared on the site of the present Schraffts Hotel and Restaurant, about 1928. (C.C.)

SUNNING, PICTURE-TAKING, BUILDING SAND CASTLES, these pastimes occupied the younger set on the popular Clearwater Beach in the sultry days of August, 1926. The cooling waters of the Gulf of Mexico refreshed bathers, while sailing and fishing entertained other folks. (P.C.H.C.)

Facing page, bottom: CLEARWATER BEACH was nearly virgin territory in 1928 when this aerial view was shot. Think what it is like today! (Burgert)

GLADIOLAS have been a big money crop in the Clearwater area since the halcyon days of the Florida boom. This was one of the large bulb farms in 1927. (P.C.H.C.)

Facing page: PALMS AND MANGROVES thrive along the shoreline and make for a beautiful scene. (Burgert)

NEIGHBORING DUNEDIN was a prosperous community in 1928. (Burgert)

Facing page: A GOOD AERIAL LOOK at Clearwater and the Memorial Causeway in March 1931. (Burgert)

Clearwater in the 1930s

ONE WAY TO FORGET THE BLUES of the depression years was to go to the inviting Clearwater Beach (*above*) and play around the old Palm Pavilion, as the folks were doing in 1930. Swimming was then followed by a visit to Joyland, the large domed building that featured slides off its high roof (*below*). (Burgert)

THERE'S A DEPRESSION ON, but one couldn't tell it from all the cars and activity going on downtown Clearwater at Cleveland Street and Garden Avenue, looking west. (Burgert)

FIFTEEN THOUSAND PERSONS saw George DeMarr, Jockey Barrett up, of the J. B. Partridge stables, streak past the finish post for the lion's share of a $1,500 purse and a $500 silver loving cup in the inaugural Handicap race of the opening day of the West Coast Jockey Club at Clearwater in the early 1930s. It ushered in a 39-day race meet, the first held on the Florida West Coast in 17 years. (P.C.H.C.)

A COMMON SCENE during the great depression from 1929 into most of the 1930s: The Relief Committee distributing Federal government flour free to local needy families at the Atlantic Coast Line Railroad depot direct from the box car. Theodore Skinner and Frank Tack were co-chairmen of this effort. (C.C.)

THE MEMORIAL CAUSEWAY to Clearwater Beach was comparatively new in 1931. When the "million dollar causeway" was built, it was as a memorial to the heroes of World War I. Turner-Brandon Post No. 7, American Legion, contributed to the project by placing two statues, those of a soldier and a sailor, at the Clearwater foot of the causeway. The soldier statue is seen here. The statues were dedicated to the men of Pinellas County who had made the supreme sacrifice, and a feature of the dedication service was the firing of a salute after each name was read. National officers of the American Legion participated in the service. The Legion Post was organized in 1919, and a year later, helped organize the Legion Post at Tarpon Springs. (P.C.H.C.)

THE IVY-COVERED Morton F. Plant Hospital was nearly 20 years old in 1931. It was named in honor of Morton F. Plant, early civic leader of Clearwater who put up the bulk of the money needed to build it in 1914. (P.C.H.C.)

LOOKING FROM CLEARWATER BEACH to the mainland across Memorial Causeway in the 1930s. Everingham's Pavilion is in the lower left hand corner of photo. (Burgert)

THE POSTMASTER GENERAL HIMSELF came down to Clearwater the day they dedicated the new U.S. Post Office on Cleveland Street in 1933. That's James A. Farley, the Postmaster General and political confidant of President Franklin D. Roosevelt, at the microphone. The ceremonies were broadcast over WSUN and WFLA. (C.C.)

ANOTHER ENGINEERING TRIUMPH was the completion of the Davis Causeway toll span across Old Tampa Bay between Clearwater and Tampa. It was the vision and dream of Captain B. T. Davis, and was opened to traffic on June 28, 1934, just 10 years after an earlier span between Tampa and Pinellas County—Gandy Bridge, also a tollway—had opened. This is an excellent aerial showing the full length of the nine and a half mile Davis project. The radio tower is that of WFLA, and the station's engineer, Joe Mitchell, lived in one of the houses in foreground. (Burgert)

～ DAVIS CAUSEWAY ～
THE QUICK, SAFE ROUTE ACROSS OLD TAMPA BAY

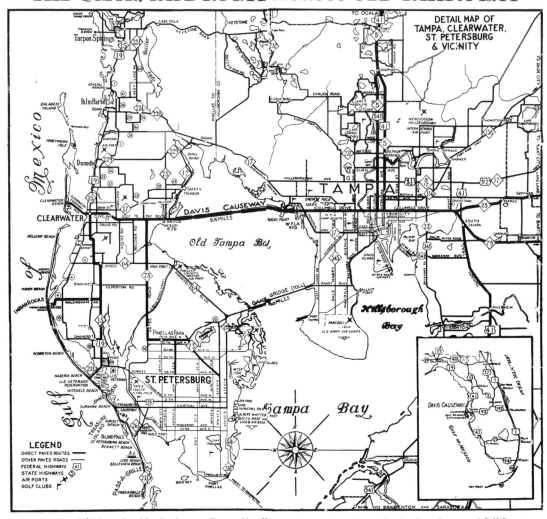

DETAIL MAP OF TAMPA, CLEARWATER, ST. PETERSBURG & VICINITY

LEGEND
DIRECT PAVED ROUTES
OTHER PAVED ROADS
FEDERAL HIGHWAYS
STATE HIGHWAYS
AIR PORTS
GOLF CLUBS

Accurate Map of Hillsborough and Pinellas Counties, Showing Main Highways, Bridges, Towns, Ferries, Beaches, Bays, Airports and Golf Courses.

Use Davis Causeway for Safety and Comfort.   ∴   Save Time, Gas, Money and Avoid Accidents

Built by B. T. Davis and opened to traffic June 28, 1934. Spans beautiful Old Tampa Bay from west shore of Hillsborough County to east shore of Pinellas County. 9½ miles long from shore to shore. — Roadway 24 feet wide, smooth, straight and well marked. Connects Tampa and mainland with Clearwater, St. Petersburg, Indian Rocks, Pass-a-Grille and other Gulf beaches.

═ TOLL RATES ═

PLEASURE		COMMERCIAL	
Auto and Driver	25c	Truck and Driver, per thousand lbs. gross	5c
Extra Passengers, each	5c	Minimum	25c
Children under 12 years	Free	Extra Passengers	5c
House Trailers, per thousand lbs.	5c		
Minimum	15c		
Trailers under 1000 lbs.	5c		
Motorcycles	10c		
Extra Passenger, each	5c		

ROUND TRIP 50c
Passenger Cars & all Passengers

TOLL GATE on the Clearwater side of Davis Causeway. The gentleman seated at the table at right was, according to the sign on his table, taking a traffic survey at the time. Tolls were collected until 1944 when the Federal government took over the span under its war powers so that military personnel could travel back and forth from MacDill Air Force Base to recreational facilities on the Gulf and to their housing on the Pinellas side. Under pressure from Uncle Sam, the owner sold the causeway to the State Road Department for $1,085,000, of which the Federal Works Administration paid half and the SRD paid the remainder. The action came during a political campaign in 1944 when then-U. S. Senator Claude Pepper, who resided in St. Petersburg at the time, was in a fight for his political life. He persuaded his close friend, President Franklin D. Roosevelt, to take over the toll spans and this paved the way for his victory. (Burgert)

CAPTAIN BEN T. DAVIS, the determined builder of Davis Causeway with his grandsons Ben C. Davis, left, and George T. Davis. The famous Davis Causeway car was known all over the state because of the Florida State Flag on the door. After World War II, the name of the span was changed to Courtney Campbell Parkway in honor of the First District Road Board member, Courtney W. Campbell, who had worked to get the approaches improved and to erect roadside parks. Campbell later was to become U. S. Congressman. The name of Captain Davis is also perpetuated in the Ben T. Davis Beach, the municipally-operated beach at the Tampa end of the causeway. (Dunn)

Facing page: DAVIS CAUSEWAY ISSUED THIS FLYER to encourage motorists to use the fine new facility connecting Tampa with Pinellas peninsula in the 1930s. The toll was 50 cents for a round trip of passenger car and all passengers. (Dunn)

AIRPLANES were still curiosity pieces back in the 1930s when a barnstorming aircraft like this one (*above*) put in at Clearwater airport, or when a Ford Trimotor (*below*) landed to disembark intrepid passengers. (P.C.H.C.)

HISTORIC ANDREWS MEMORIAL CHAPEL in Dunedin is a landmark in the religious life of Pinellas County. In May, 1868, The Rev. Joseph Brown came by schooner to Dunedin and started Ebenezer Church, the parent church of the First Presbyterian Church of Dunedin. It later was called Bethesda Church and, since 1878, Andrews Memorial Church. The chapel is said to be the oldest church building in the county. Only one other building in Dunedin, the railroad station, is known to be older. The chapel was preserved in the 1970s by the Dunedin Historical Society. (Dunn)

A WATER SPRITE, or happiness is dancing through the surf of the cooling Gulf of Mexico at Clearwater Beach. (Wyngarden)

AN ENCHANTING SCENE on the Anclote River near Tarpon Springs. (Burgert)

THE POST OFFICE was in the Scranton Arcade for many years. The stores were occupied by Ray Green Drug Store, Rellops Dress Shop, Postal Telegraph, Dutch Kitchen, *St. Petersburg Times*, Children's Shoppe, Hardin and Shaw Barber Shop, and Frank J. Booth Real Estate. The Arcade was at the southeast corner of Cleveland Street and Garden Avenue. (C.C.)

BUSY DOWNTOWN CLEARWATER in 1934. (P.C.H.C.)

THE CLEARWATER CITY HALL was an attractive brick structure in the mid-1930s. (P.C.H.C.)

THE POST OFFICE on Cleveland Street was nearly new in 1935 when this photo was made. The traffic on the main drag was certainly heavy! (P.C.H.C.)

PEOPLE CAME in large numbers when the 1935 Regatta was held. Automobiles are lining the waterside (*above*), while boating enthusiasts are jamming both sides of the channel (*below*). (Wyngarden)

Mischief LEADS *Jay Dee II* in the 1935 Regatta in Clearwater. (Wyngarden)

CLEARWATER HIGH SCHOOL FOOT-BALL action (*below* and *right*) in the mid-1930s thrilled the crowds. Cecil Reed (*left*), a star end for the Clearwater High School Tornadoes, went on to be a standout player for the University of Tampa Spartans. (Wyngarden)

CLEARWATER GOT ITS OWN RADIO STATION in the mid-1930s when Mayor Ham Baskin, Walter Tison, and a corporation bought WFLA which previously had been a twin operation using WSUN call letters from St. Petersburg and WFLA from Clearwater. The *Tampa Tribune* took over the corporation and the station in 1938. On may 1, 1941, the Tribune went full-time under the call letters WFLA. Photos on this page show WFLA's studios in its earlier days, as well as its control room. (Burgert)

CLERKS IN THE COURT HOUSE were busy on some special project in this scene in the old Circuit Court Room in the Pinellas County Court House on May 27, 1936. (Burgert)

THE CLEARWATER LIONS CLUB and guests in front of the Clearwater Yacht Club in 1936. Many past and present of Clearwater's business leaders are in the picture. (C.C.)

THE CLEARWATER YACHT CLUB in 1936 just after the top floor of the old beach pavilion was moved across Mandalay Road to become the club house. (C.C.)

SAFETY HARBOR continued to be a fine health resort (*above*) in 1936, and most of the activities centered around the Spa. *Below*: The lobby of the popular Spa. The famed springs were downstairs. (Burgert)

ST. NICHOLAS GREEK ORTHODOX CHURCH on Orange Street between Hibiscus Street and Pinellas Avenue in the heart of Tarpon Springs is literally in the hearts of all who live here. Someone has noted that St. Nicholas is the very center, "the mortar," of Greek community life. The sponge industry developed here at the turn of the century, and professional divers were imported from Greece. By 1903, the town began celebrating Epiphany Day on January 6, one of the most holy days of the Greek Orthodox Church. In the same year, the first St. Nicholas Church was started. It was finished in 1907, a small edifice seating only 250 persons and costing $15,000, which is quite in contrast to the gorgeous and elegant cathedral that was dedicated in 1941. (Dunn)

ON EPIPHANY DAY, rites are first conducted in the church. The beautiful Byzantine structure has a glistening interior of white Grecian marble which serves to highlight the magnificent beauty of stained glass windows and iconography, offset by several huge, delicate crystal chandeliers. A white Carrara-marble altar is dedicated to the memory of the Rev. Theophilos Kara-phillis who served in the church as pastor from 1922 until his death in 1963. (Burgert)

THOUSANDS OF THE DEVOUT as well as tourists throng the banks of Spring Bayou in 1937 (*above*) to watch the fishermen dive for the gilded cross that the Archbishop will toss into the water shortly. The excitement rises as the Archbishop arrives aboard the platform raft on Epiphany Day to toss the cross into the cold water (*below*). Colorful decorations and bright native Greek costumes add to the glamor of the occasion. (Burgert)

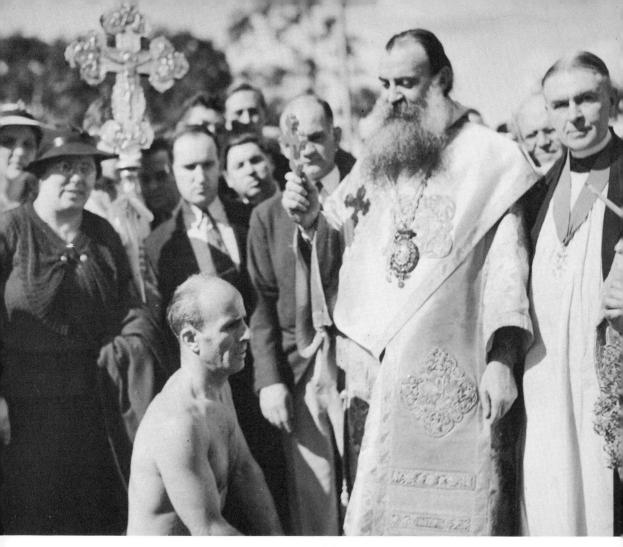

A SPECIAL BLESSING by the Archbishop for the lucky retriever of the golden cross (*above*) that will bring him good luck throughout the following year, an honor much coveted by the men of Tarpon Springs. Here is the scene one year back in the 1930s as the Archbishop blessed the recipient. Humble, yet proud is the devotion of the winner of 1941 (*right*) as he climbs on the raft to receive the blessing. (Burgert)

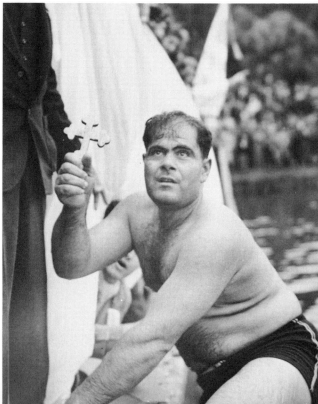

THE TARPON SPRINGS SPONGE EX-
CHANGE (*above*) did not appear too
busy that day in 1936 when this over-
view of the vast operation was taken. A
sponge diver preparing to dive dons the
heavy, equipment and diving suit (*left*)
needed to go beneath the waters to
collect sponges. (Burgert)

[131]

THEY WERE HAVING A BEAUTY CONTEST in 1937 when these lovelies gathered at the Clearwater Carlouel for a bit of relaxation before the big event. The fortunate gentleman in the foreground at right is Taver Bayly. (Burgert)

A LITTLE TOO YOUNG for beauty contests are these cute little tykes who appreciate the white, sandy beaches of Clearwater as much as the grownups do, even if the bright sunshine makes them squint. (Wyngarden)

WHO DOESN'T LIKE a relaxing, fun-filled day at Clearwater Beach? (Burgert)

IT'S A FAMILY AFFAIR, going to the beach at Clearwater! (Burgert)

AQUAPLANING IN THE GULF OF MEXICO (*above*) was a popular sport in Clearwater during the
depression years, and if done late in the afternoon, would let you witness a spectacular, yet typical
sunset (*below*). (Burgert)

Clearwater since 1940

THE WEST COAST HOTEL at Clearwater was new as 1940 dawned. War clouds were gathering over the nation at the time. (Burgert)

HOMECOMING AT HISTORIC ANONA CHURCH brought out these pioneers in October, 1940. In 1872, settlers of a community known as Lowe's Landing held their first church services since the area was settled 13 years earlier. A circuit rider, the Rev. John Wells, conducted services in the home of a Mrs. Woodward. In the course of the following century, Lowe's Landing took on the name Anona, which later was incorporated into Largo. The Anona United Methodist Church celebrated its 100th anniversary in 1972. (P.C.H.C.)

"OH, SAY CAN YOU SEE?"—the National Anthem was often heard during the stirring days of the early 1940s while Clearwater and the rest of the country prepared for entry in World War II. (Burgert)

Preceding page: CLEARWATER FROM THE AIR in 1940—the Fort Harrison Hotel dominates the foreground, the Calvary Baptist Church is beyond the hotel to the right and toward the causeway that leads to Clearwater Beach. (P.C.H.C.)

DURING WORLD WAR II, 1941-45, U. S. Army and Air Force personnel occupied hotels in the Clearwater area. They drilled in these streets and daily raised the Stars and Stripes in front of the Pinellas County Court House. (P.C.H.C.)

THEY SOLD A LOT OF U. S. WAR BONDS during a World War II Bond Rally featuring the U. S. Marine Band in front of Clearwater's Capitol Theatre. "We over-subscribed each time!" is the proud boast of the community about war bond sales. As the marquee shows, persons purchasing war bonds were admitted to the "Gala War Bond Premier" of "DuBarry Was a Lady." The former Chamber of Commerce building is next door to the theatre. (C.C.)

THE AMPHIBIAN "ALLIGATOR" used in World War II for island invasions in the Pacific and elsewhere was invented right here in Clearwater by Donald Roebling. The jubilant lads aboard in this picture were Boy Scouts and Sea Scouts of the Clearwater area. (C.C.)

IT WASN'T ALL WORK and no play for the soldiers, sailors, and airmen training here during World War II. For instance, there were those gala dances at the Clearwater Auditorium featuring the Grand March shown here. (P.C.H.C.)

CLEARWATER SEA SCOUTS entertained themselves while learning skills of seamanship. (Wyngarden)

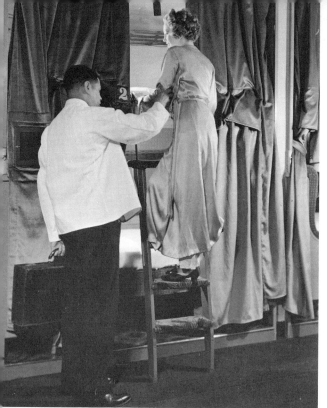

TRAVEL BY TRAIN was the màin mode of transportation during World War II. Here a Pullman porter assists a lady passenger to her upper berth. (Wyngarden)

"I CHRISTEN THEE *S. S. Clearwater Victory*" says Miss Vicky Morgan (*below*) as she smashes champagne over the bow of the World War II ship (*right*) at Richmond, Calif. shipyards on January 20, 1945. As sign indicates, it was the 584th ship built by the Permanente Metals Corporation. (P.C.H.C.)

CLEARWATER FIRST HAD TELEPHONE in 1900, and the system expanded through the years. This was Peninsular Telephone Company's Clearwater Building, at the corner of Garden and Cleveland, in 1947. The toll board and switchboard were on the second floor, and the commercial office was on the ground floor at the rear. Peninsular was the predecessor to General Telephone Company of Florida. (General Telephone Co.)

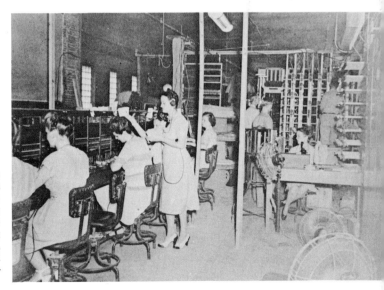

THE CRUSH OF EXPANSION in the telephone industry after World War II is apparent in this photograph taken in the Peninsular Telephone Company building in Clearwater. Operators continued to work while the toll room was being remodeled and new equipment installed, paying little attention to the noise and activity around them. (General Telephone Co.)

[143]

THE OLD SUNSET HILLS COUNTRY CLUB in Tarpon Springs, which was built during the fabulous Florida real estate boom of the 1920s, was turned into a fine resort hotel, called The Upham House on the Gulf of Mexico, after World War II. John Upham, an insurance executive from Des Moines, Iowa, renovated the building, and built a cocktail lounge and a swimming pool. He operated it for several years, but finally closed it. The splendid facility is now the hospital of the Anclote Psychiatric Center. (Anclote)

THE SPONGE MARKET and vicinity in Tarpon Springs, the charming Greek-American community, in 1947. (Burgert)

CLEARWATER in 1947. (Burgert)

AN ATTRACTIVE ESTATE in Eagle's Nest at Belleair in 1945. (Burgert)

"THE WHITE QUEEN OF THE GULF," the fabulous Belleview Biltmore Hotel, housed U. S. Air Force men during World War II, and reopened for regular guests after the war. It is still in operation. (Dunn)

THE ENTIRE FAMILY ENJOYS an outing on the Courtney Campbell Parkway between Clearwater and Tampa where there are picnic tables and stoves for preparing food. Youngsters swim, and oldsters try their luck at fishing. (Burgert)

SHUFFLEBOARD IS THE TOP SPORT for most winter visitors to the Florida Gulf Coast. Here's some of the action at the Clearwater Beach Hotel right on the beach. (Burgert)

CLEARWATER HAS NEVER BEEN SHORT of beauties to compete in beauty contests—here's a bevy of them in the 1950s. (Burgert)

POPULAR CLEARWATER BEACH in 1949: Men were wearing topless suits by then, and the ladies were daring in their two-piece suits. (Burgert)

THE SURF WAS HIGH on March 26, 1952, and the springtime crowds were streaming to Clearwater Beach. (Burgert)

THE MAGNIFICENT MARINA on Clearwater Beach was built in the 1950s, a facility welcomed by all yachtsmen of the West coast. (Burgert)

THE POPULATION EXPLOSION brought about real estate development in Clearwater as elsewhere. *Above* is an aerial view of Skycrest, a gladiolus farm before its conversion into an attractive residential subdivision (*below*) in the early 1950s. (Wyngarden)

CLEVELAND STREET in downtown Clearwater in 1952, looking toward the Causeway. (Burgert)

PINELLAS OLD-TIMERS CELEBRATE the fortieth anniversary of the county in January 1952. Here are Chester Bartow MacMullen, State Attorney and later U. S. Congressman; Dixie M. Hollins, first County School Superintendent in 1912; and Melvin A. McMullen, Circuit Judge. (P.C.H.C.)

MODERN VIEW of the Belleview-Biltmore Hotel. The largest wooden structure under one roof, the hotel overlooks Clearwater Bay. The two Donald J. Ross championship golf courses are just steps away. Containing 400 rooms, the hotel has more than two miles of corridors and requires 1,000 gallons of paint for one exterior coat. (Dunn)

YOU'D NEVER RECOGNIZE IT NOW, but this was Ozona near Dunedin in June 1950. Even then pumping was going on, and the community was beginning its phenomenal growth. (Burgert)

A DRUG STORE EMPIRE was born on Cleveland Street in 1952 when Jack M. Eckerd acquired the little store next to McCrory's and launched his business. He also picked up a couple of small stores in Tampa about the same time. Those three stores, with 19 employees, constituted the nucleus of today's Jack Eckerd Corporation which, with almost 8,000 employees, operates close to 300 Eckerd Drug Stores in five states, 23 department stores, a food service equipment and supply firm, and a security services company. Eckerd entered his family's drug store business in Erie, Pennsylvania, in 1932, and went to work in the basement stockroom. Just 20 years later, and after service as a pilot in World War II, he had left the business in Erie, moved to Wilmington, Delaware, and five years later to Florida. When he began his chain, the retail druggists were undergoing a major transition in their service to customers. Aside from their prescription departments, drug stores, en masse, were cutting back on clerks and switching over to a complete self-service. "We took a different tack," Eckerd recalls, and went down the middle. We decided to offer self-service in some departments, but to maintain a staff of carefully trained clerks in such departments as non-prescription drugs and cosmetics, where customers often need and appreciate service and advice." (Burgert)

JACK ECKERD, who lives in Belleair, entered politics and ran for Governor of Florida in 1970 on the Republican ticket. He eliminated L. A. "Skip" Bafalis in the first primary and battled the incumbent Governor, Claude Kirk, in the runoff. Kirk won with approximately 200,000 votes to Eckerd's 152,000, but lost out to Democrat Reubin Askew in the general election. The drug store king has been active in civic affairs of Clearwater and of Florida. He perpetuated his name with gifts totaling $12.5 million to the old Florida Presbyterian College, in St. Petersburg, which changed its name in 1972 to Eckerd College.

CLEARWATER LONG HAS BEEN FAMOUS for its superior golf courses, ever since Henry B. Plant built the Belleview Hotel at Belleair in 1896 and featured the game at that resort. *Above* is the pretty tee No. 5 on the old Clearwater Country Club. The scene (*below*) at the 9th and 18th greens evoked fond memories in Clearwater attorney Bill Boza who is also a local historian. (Burgert)

THE CARLOUEL YACHT CLUB on Clearwater Beach (*above*) with its handsome lobby (*right*) and its popular dining room. The architect for the building was Ray W. Wakeling. (Burgert)

THE QUIET COMMUNITY OF DUNEDIN shared in the growth of the 1950s, and the Chamber of Commerce (*above*) was as important in Dunedin's development as was its bank (*below*). (Burgert)

THE BOOM-TIME FENWAY HOTEL at Dunedin, shown here in the 1950s, was to become the home of Trinity College, a Bible institute, in 1960. It was an elegant resort during the Florida real estate heyday but was shuttered during the depression. Trinity College was born as Florida Bible College during the early 1930s and first operated in the old Temple Terrace Country Club, at nearby Tampa. One of the students at the school in Tampa was the famed evangelist Billy Graham, then a gangling, frightened teen-ager. He graduated from Trinity in the class of 1940. During World War II, the college [159] moved to a defunct private club at Belleair, and then to Dunedin in 1960. Alumnus Graham has remembered his Alma Mater: He gave a $10,000 gift to the school and a building on the campus is named in his honor, called the Billy Graham Hall of Evangelism. (Burgert)

WATCH THAT WATER HAZARD! The golf course at Dunedin in the early 1950s. (Burgert)

ONE QUICK GLIMPSE of downtown Clearwater in the 1960s—progress marches on. (Burgert)